Prayers

for your

Fasting Journey

Vernet Clemons Nettles

Published by: VCNettles Inspirations and Letters
www.vernetcnettles.com
vernetcnettles@gmail.com

Scripture from The Holy Bible, New King James Version (NKJV), Copyright 1982 Thomas Nelson.

Cover Design: Elite Book Covers

ISBN: 978-1-959543-13-8

Printed in the United States

Acknowledgements

I am so thrilled to always be able to say **THANK YOU to my family** who always support and read with me.

A special thank you to Rev. James and Rev. T'dera, two irreplaceable mentors; and Rev. GWC, whose voice still rings in my heart.

Thank you to the Holy Spirit, who continuously nudged me to finish this prayer journey. I understand now. There are many of us (and yes, I am including myself) who desire to pray, but can't always find a focus or guidance. These prayers provide the focus, your heart and the Holy Spirit will fill in the gaps.

And thank YOU – the reader. Thank you for your purchase. It is my prayer that the Holy Spirit speaks to you through these words and that your prayer-walk and journey is and always will be WONDERFUL!

Table of Contents

"And do not be conformed to this world, but be transformed by the renewing of your mind, that you may prove what is that good and acceptable and perfect will of God."

Romans 12:2 NKJV

A Fasting Experience

Prayers for Your Fasting Journey is not written to teach anyone how to fast or whether to fast. By definition, a fast is the voluntary elimination of certain food or drink for a specific time or purpose. There are multiple reasons to fast; often those reasons are spiritual or health related.

This book is written to accompany you on your journey if you decide to participate in a fast and/or prayer journey. It is my hope that these prayers will provide focus and guidance during your period of fasting.

The very first time I actually prepared myself for and completed a fast was only a few years ago. My church had gone on January Fasts for many years. Every January, I expected my pastor's booming voice to not only announce the corporate fast, but to also announce that upon the end of the fast, he was planning to have possum or coon (or some other insane dish that he wasn't ever supposed to eat). The congregation would laugh, and they would get started.

My pastor would talk about corporate fasting, in which the church-body would fast for the vision of the church, or the family-unit would fast for the vison of the family. But he would also encourage us to personally fast and to ask God for the direction He desires for our lives during the new year.

It was all very inspiring. But yes, I said "they." Because I either didn't always understand the process, or I didn't think I had the fortitude, discipline, or praying ability to maintain for 21 days, let alone 30 days.

But one year, I felt brave and decided to give it a try. I was pleasantly surprised. Not only did I have the discipline, but I also needed the prayer time. That year several things I had been praying and whining about (full transparency) began to take focus. The bonus - I even lost a few pounds.

That year, I realized that fasting is not so much about the food you shouldn't eat or what you take away. It is more about what you add to your life

- the prayer-walk and the focus on what God desires for your life. It was the active listening with your heart and soul that was new for me. It was the realization that words I spoke or wrote – that I had never spoken or written before – were a manifestation of the time spent with God during the fast.

As fasting practices have continued, many have determined that there are other things that can be eliminated for focused time in prayer. If you're like me, not only food and sweets, but cell phone time and television programs are emotional soothers and time guzzlers. These activities can often result in time 'wasted' that many of us need to focus our energies on what is important, to recreate our personal synergies, or very simply, to begin to focus more on our Christian walk and relationship with God.

Truth be told, sometimes the fast is promoted as a cure-all. It is not. A fast is an opportunity to release some worldly distractions (temporarily or permanently) so that there is more deliberate focus on self, health, or most importantly, our walk with God.

Transparency. When I participated in the first fast, I was unsure of how to pray or what to pray for. So, I whispered some words and kept pushing: "Lord, what is your plan for my church and my life this year?" Over the years, however, I have wanted to have more focused and meaningful prayers during my fasting periods.

One year, my sisters and I prayed the same prayers most days of the fast period. One of us would text the prayer to the others. Knowing that we were praying together, I believe that the prayers helped me to focus my prayer time. I hope this book of prayers does the same for you.

More transparency. The limitation of certain foods or the restrictions of certain activities can be daunting. However, we must be reminded that the purpose of participating in a fast is to grow closer to God. We get so afraid that if we make a mistake, miss a prayer time, or eat the wrong food, we have not completed the fast correctly or we will miss Christ's blessings. Then, we give up. Not So. If you slip up, get back to it. It's like our Christian walk. We slip up; repent; start over, and renew ourselves. Please know that my comments are not designed to make light of this religious practice; however, fasting is the activity; the connection to God is our Goal.

Let us Pray.

"Be anxious for nothing, but in everything by prayer and supplication, with thanksgiving, let your requests be made known to God; and the peace of God, which surpasses all understanding, will guard your hearts and minds through Christ Jesus."

Philippians 4:6-7 NKJV

Three Examples of Fasting in the Bible

"So he [Moses] was there with the Lord forty days and forty nights; he neither ate bread nor drank water. And He wrote on the tablets the words of the covenant, the Ten Commandments."

Exodus 34:28 NKJV

"Go, gather all the Jews who are present in Shushan, and fast for me; neither eat nor drink for three days, night or day. My maids and I will fast likewise. And so, I will go to the king, which is against the law; and if I perish, I perish!"

Esther 4:16 NKJV

"Then Jesus was led up by the Spirit into the wilderness to be tempted by the devil. And when He had fasted forty days and forty nights, afterward He was hungry."

Matthew 4:1-2 NKJV

Disclaimer

This book is written as a ***Prayer Journey*** - a set of prayers to accompany the reader when time is set aside to focus on prayer.

If you choose to fast, here are 21 prayers to help you focus your prayers for ***guidance and revelation.***

This book, however, is not written to promote fasting. Although there are many variations of fasting, ***please consult with your physician(s)*** before beginning any type fast to determine if this is appropriate for your health journey, especially if you have a medical condition.

And if all is well...

> ***Let Us Pray...***

Heart to Heart...

At the top of each Reflection page are two hearts. The two hearts represent (1) your heart lifted to God; and (2) my heart praying with yours.

"Two are better than one, Because they have a good reward for their labor. For if they fall, one will lift up his companion....

Ecclesiastes 4:9-10a NKJV

If you would like to communicate during your Fasting and/or Prayer Journey, I would love to pray with you. Please feel free to email me at vcnprayerjourney@gmail.com

One More Thing...

We vs I   Us vs Me

In my writing, I often pray in the collective. I do so, because I believe that when we pray, we should pray for others and ourselves.

BUT, I encourage you as you read to insert the individual for the collective. Feel the power of your personal journey. Then, pray again in the collective, as we seek the promise for us all.

"Again, I say to you that if two of you agree on earth concerning anything that they ask, it will be done for them by My Father in heaven. For where two or three are gathered together in My name, I am there in the midst of them."

Matthew 18:19-20 NKJV

Prayers
for your
Fasting Journey

Preparation:

"Now, therefore," says the Lord, "Turn to Me with all your heart, With fasting, with weeping, and with mourning." So rend your heart, and not your garments; Return to the Lord your God, For He is gracious and merciful, Slow to anger, and of great kindness; And He relents from doing harm."

Joel 2:12-13 NKJV

Heavenly Father, thank you for all things, for your voice that speaks and calls to me. I bring to you my contrite heart. I desire to hear your voice and feel your love that welcomes me back to you. In Jesus' name we pray. *Amen.*

Prayer Day 1

"O God, You are my God; Early will I seek You; My soul thirsts for You; My flesh longs for You In a dry and thirsty land Where there is no water."

Psalm 63:1 NKJV

Heavenly Father, thank you for your many blessings, your grace, your mercy, and your love. As we begin this 21-day fasting and/or prayer journey, we ask for focus on you and clarity from you. Guide us. Grant us discernment to hear from you as you whisper your plans for our lives. Lord, we love you, we thank you, and we look forward to what you will reveal to us - individually and collectively. In Jesus' name we pray and begin again with You. *Amen.*

Reflections

1. As you begin this prayer journey what are you seeking?

   _____

   _____

   _____

   _____

2. What / How are you hearing from God today?

   _____

   _____

   _____

   _____

3. What is your personal prayer for today?

   _____

   _____

   _____

   _____

   _____

Prayer Day 2

"I will stand my watch And set myself on the rampart, And watch to see what He will say to me, And what I will answer when I am corrected. Then the LORD answered me and said: "Write the vision And make it plain on tablets, That he may run who reads it."

Habakkuk 2:1-2 NKJV

Father God, thank you for today. Thank you for another day to focus on you during this fast. Thank you for this time to listen even more closely to what you are saying. Remind us, Lord, to write down the vision. Lord, our memories are not what they used to be, help us to hold on to your thoughts until we get to a piece of paper to write them down. In Jesus' name we pray and praise. *Amen.*

Reflections

1. What is your vision (or the vision you are seeking) that you are focusing on during this prayer journey?

   _____

   _____

   _____

   _____

2. What / How are you hearing from God today?

   _____

   _____

   _____

   _____

3. What is your personal prayer for today?

   _____

   _____

   _____

   _____

Prayer Day 3

"There are many plans in a man's heart, Nevertheless the Lord's counsel—that will stand."

Proverbs 19:21 NKJV

Father God, thank you for reminding us to seek your counsel. We are always planning our lives. During this period of prayer, we seek your counsel. Reveal to us the plans you have for our lives for such a time as this. Allow us to know our purpose so that the work we do impacts the building of your kingdom. Allow us to see the tools you have placed within us to fulfill your plans for us. In Jesus' name we pray and listen. *Amen.*

Reflections

1. What plans are you praying about? What clarity are you seeking?

   _____

   _____

   _____

   _____

2. What / How are you hearing from God today?

   _____

   _____

   _____

   _____

3. What is your personal prayer for today?

   _____

   _____

   _____

   _____

   _____

Prayer Day 4

"For I know the thoughts that I think toward you, says the Lord, thoughts of peace and not of evil, to give you a future and a hope."

Jeremiah 29:11 NKJV

Gracious Father, thank you for reminding us of purpose. Continue, Father, during this fast to reveal to us your purpose for our lives. Help us to see the seed that you planted in us. Remind us to nurture and grow that seed to its fruition. In Jesus' name we pray and praise. **Amen.**

> **Hmmm**...*I was reminded that we have God given talent - which is the seed that must be nourished. We must train, practice, and pray about our talent, so that the seed can blossom and grow.*

Reflections

1. What seeds do you feel God has planted in you? How are you nurturing them?

   _____

   _____

   _____

   _____

2. What / How are you hearing from God today?

   _____

   _____

   _____

   _____

3. What is your personal prayer for today?

   _____

   _____

   _____

   _____

   _____

Prayer Day 5

"No temptation has overtaken you except such as is common to man; but God is faithful, who will not allow you to be tempted beyond what you are able, but with the temptation will also make the way of escape, that you may be able to bear it."

I Corinthians 10:13 NKJV

Wonderful Father, thank you for opportunities for activities of fun and down time. Forgive us for becoming so engrossed in our down time that the fun becomes a distraction. Father, grant us the will to identify and put down our distractions so that we can focus on our purpose and our _____. Grant us peace in our spirits from the need to drown ourselves in meaningless tasks to escape the world. Strengthen us for the journey. In Jesus' name we pray. *Amen.*

Reflections

1. What activities do you use to drown out life? Are they purposeful? Can you choose something else?

_____

_____

_____

_____

2. What / How are you hearing from God today?

_____

_____

_____

_____

3. What is your personal prayer for today?

_____

_____

_____

_____

_____

Prayer Day 6

"A friend loves at all times, And a brother is born for adversity."

Proverbs 17:17 NKJV

"As iron sharpens iron, So a man sharpens the countenance of his friend."

Proverbs 27:17 NKJV

Good Lord, thank you. Thank you for creating connections and placing new people in our lives. As we pray for purpose and peace during this fast, open our eyes, ears, and heart to recognize the people and opportunities you have placed in our lives to love us forward. Grant us the discernment to be aware of the shift and the connecting forces. Thank you, Lord. In Jesus' name we pray and praise. ***Amen.***

Reflections

1. Are you aware of the people in your life who sharpen you? Do you spend too much time with those who do not?

   _____

   _____

   _____

   _____

2. What / How are you hearing from God today?

   _____

   _____

   _____

   _____

3. What is your personal prayer for today?

   _____

   _____

   _____

   _____

   _____

Prayer Day 7

"Then you will call upon Me and go and pray to Me, and I will listen to you. And you will seek Me and find Me, when you search for Me with all your heart. I will be found by you, says the Lord, and I will bring you back from your captivity; ..."

Jeremiah 29:12-14a NKJV

Heavenly Father, thank you for your grace. Father, thank you for reminding us to seek opportunities to hear your Word. When we have the opportunity, we ask that you open our hearts so that we may receive the words that you have for us. Thank you for a Word that blesses our soul, teaches us, and prepares us for our purpose. In Jesus' name we pray and listen. ***Amen.***

Reflections

1. When you call on God, what do you expect? How do you poise yourself to hear from Him?

   _____

   _____

   _____

   _____

2. What / How are you hearing from God today?

   _____

   _____

   _____

   _____

3. What is your personal prayer for today?

   _____

   _____

   _____

   _____

   _____

Prayer Day 8

"The Lord is near to all who call upon Him, To all who call upon Him in truth. He will fulfill the desire of those who fear Him; He also will hear their cry and save them."

Psalms 145:18-19 NKJV

***

Father, thank you. So often during our storms of life, the winds howl, the rain drenches, and the electricity in the lightning makes it hard to breathe. Sometimes the power just goes out. It is during these times that we begin to feel disconnected from you - Our Source. Lord, we pray that during this fast we are and have been able to sit still and focus on your plans for our lives - so that we are reconnected and the presence of your power returns. In Jesus' name we pray and praise you in advance. ***Amen.***

Reflections

1. Have you been in a place in your life when you did not think God was listening? What did you do? Did it work?

   _____

   _____

   _____

   _____

2. What / How are you hearing from God today?

   _____

   _____

   _____

   _____

3. What is your personal prayer for today?

   _____

   _____

   _____

   _____

   _____

Prayer Day 9

"As each one has received a gift, minister it to one another, as good stewards of the manifold grace of God. If anyone speaks, let him speak as the oracles of God. If anyone ministers, let him do it as with the ability which God supplies, that in all things God may be glorified through Jesus Christ, to whom belong the glory and the dominion forever and ever. Amen."

I Peter 4:10-11 NKJV

My Lord, thank you. Thank you for your trust with the gifts you have given us. Thank you for pouring your spirit into our gifts. Father, teach us to minister with our God-given gifts to be a part of the upbuilding of your kingdom. Your word reminds us that we do things with the ability that You provide. In Jesus' name we pray and glorify your name. *Amen.*

Reflections

1. Are you using your God-given talents in some type of ministry or service? Why or why not?

_____

_____

_____

_____

2. What / How are you hearing from God today?

_____

_____

_____

_____

3. What is your personal prayer for today?

_____

_____

_____

_____

_____

Prayer Day 10

"Or do you not know that your body is the temple of the Holy Spirit who is in you, whom you have from God, and you are not your own? For you were bought at a price; therefore glorify God in your body and in your spirit, which are God's."

I Corinthians 6:19-20 NKJV

Heavenly Father, your word says that our bodies are your temples. Grant us the courage and the strength to take care of ourselves, our mental, physical, and spiritual health. Father, it is often a challenge to put ourselves first when we are always taking care of others. Help us to understand that a "Yes" to our self-care ultimately helps us continue to be of service in the future. In Jesus' name we pray. *Amen.*

Reflections

1. Are you treating your body like a temple? How or why not?

    _____

    _____

    _____

    _____

2. What / How are you hearing from God today?

    _____

    _____

    _____

    _____

3. What is your personal prayer for today?

    _____

    _____

    _____

    _____

    _____

Prayer Day 11

"If any of you lacks wisdom, let him ask of God, who gives to all liberally and without reproach, and it will be given to him. But let him ask in faith, with no doubting, for he who doubts is like a wave of the sea driven and tossed by the wind."

James 1:5-6 NKJV

Wonderful Counselor, we plan and prepare many things. But we are reminded to seek you first for guidance, wisdom, and provision for each leg of the journey. We come to you during this fast, asking for guidance, wisdom, courage, and strength to hear what you have for us on this leg of the journey and more. In Jesus' name we pray. ***Amen.***

Reflections

1. You are at the halfway mark, what are you seeking God for?

   _____

   _____

   _____

   _____

2. What / How are you hearing from God today?

   _____

   _____

   _____

   _____

3. What is your personal prayer for today?

   _____

   _____

   _____

   _____

   _____

Prayer Day 12

"Then I set my face toward the Lord God to make request by prayer and supplications, with fasting, sackcloth, and ashes. And I prayed to the Lord my God, and made confession, and said, "O Lord, great and awesome God, who keeps His covenant and mercy with those who love Him, and with those who keep His commandments,"

Daniel 9:3-4 NKJV

Heavenly Father, thank you for your loving kindness and your mercy. Forgive us our sins, our willful neglect of each other, and our _____. Thank you for your Word that teaches us to be honest with you and pour out our hearts. We know that you know our hearts, but your Word reminds us to still talk with you. Thank you, Lord, for your Word that continues to teach us. In Jesus' name we pray. ***Amen.***

Reflections

1. What do you want to thank God for? What do you want to talk to Him about?

    _____

    _____

    _____

    _____

2. What / How are you hearing from God today?

    _____

    _____

    _____

    _____

3. What is your personal prayer for today?

    _____

    _____

    _____

    _____

    _____

Prayer Day 13

"And when He had come into the house, His disciples asked Him privately, "Why could we not cast it out?" So He said to them, "This kind can come out by nothing but prayer and fasting."

Mark 9:28-29 NKJV

Our Father and Our Keeper, thank you for teaching us to remain connected to you in prayer; for teaching us to rely on you in all situations; and for reminding us that sometimes, it is our consistent and fervent prayers that will change things. Thank you, Lord. In Jesus' name we pray and praise. ***Amen.***

Hmmm...We spend so much time trying to create change under our own power. We cannot cast "it" out without prayer - which is our connection to Christ.

Reflections

1. Are you a person who consistently prays? Why or why not?

   _____

   _____

   _____

   _____

2. What / How are you hearing from God today?

   _____

   _____

   _____

   _____

3. What is your personal prayer for today?

   _____

   _____

   _____

   _____

   _____

Prayer Day 14

"Of the birds after their kind, of animals after their kind, and of every creeping thing of the earth after its kind, two of every kind will come to you to keep them alive."

Genesis 6:20 NKJV

***

Our Father, thank you for reminding us that when you charge us with purpose, you also provide opportunities for the task to manifest - the animals came to the ark. Forgive us for worrying – how, when, and where. Help us to rest in the joy of the assignment and the promise that you are placing things in order. Thank you, Lord, for your gift of a plan. In Jesus' name we pray and praise. *Amen.*

Hmmm…God sent the animals to the ark; Noah did not have to go find them. When God gives you an assignment, there may be challenges, but many opportunities will come to you. Wait on Him.

Reflections

1. Do you worry a lot? Have you noticed that God can put things in order better than when you worry? What did you discover?

   _____

   _____

   _____

   _____

2. What / How are you hearing from God today?

   _____

   _____

   _____

   _____

3. What is your personal prayer for today?

   _____

   _____

   _____

   _____

   _____

Prayer Day 15

"Now, therefore," says the LORD, "Turn to Me with all your heart, With fasting, with weeping, and with mourning." So rend your heart, and not your garments; Return to the LORD your God, For He is gracious and merciful, Slow to anger, and of great kindness; And He relents from doing harm."

Joel 2:12-13 NKJV

Heavenly Father, thank you for all things - for beckoning me to return to you, to your care, and to your love. Father, we turn to you, not in symbolic gestures, but we bring our hearts to you - open to receive. Thank you for your mercy and compassion. Forgive us our sins, our stubbornness, our _____. Show us a better way, so that we do not rest in our own understanding. We love you; we wait for you. In Jesus' name we pray and return to you. ***Amen.***

Reflections

1. During the fast and moving forward what do you want to release and not pick up again?

    _____

    _____

    _____

    _____

2. What / How are you hearing from God today?

    _____

    _____

    _____

    _____

3. What is your personal prayer for today?

    _____

    _____

    _____

    _____

    _____

Prayer Day 16

"The disciples of John and of the Pharisees were fasting. Then they came and said to Him, "Why do the disciples of John and of the Pharisees fast, but Your disciples do not fast?" And Jesus said to them, "Can the friends of the bridegroom fast while the bridegroom is with them? As long as they have the bridegroom with them they cannot fast. But the days will come when the bridegroom will be taken away from them, and then they will fast in those days."

Mark 2:18-20 NKJV

Heavenly Father, thank you for all things. Father, thank you for teaching us the purpose of fasting. Thank you for teaching us that the purpose of fasting is to draw closer to you, to seek understanding and guidance from you, and to seek your presence in our lives. Father, we glorify you, we seek you in our lives, we thirst for you. In Jesus' name we pray. *Amen.*

Reflections

1. Have you been able to draw closer to Christ during this fast? How and/or why not? And if why not, what other steps can you take?

_____

_____

_____

_____

2. What / How are you hearing from God today?

_____

_____

_____

_____

3. What is your personal prayer for today?

_____

_____

_____

_____

_____

Prayer Day 17

"Therefore, if you died with Christ from the basic principles of the world, why, as though living in the world, do you subject yourselves to regulations—"Do not touch, do not taste, do not handle," which all concern things which perish with the using—according to the commandments and doctrines of men? These things indeed have an appearance of wisdom in self-imposed religion, false humility, and neglect of the body, but are of no value against the indulgence of the flesh."

Colossians 2:20-23 NKJV

My Lord, Our God, thank you for your timely points of clarity. Thank you for reminding us that rules and traditions do not save us. Forgive us for clinging to old traditions and expectations. Help us to focus on our daily walk with you. Remind us to be kind, to be just, and to be loving toward others - as you have loved us. Keep us in your keeping care. In Jesus' name we pray. **Amen.**

Hmmm...This scripture confirms and clarifies. It signals for us to think about why we do things. Our actions alone of self-denial will not save us. We should focus on our faith and Our Jesus. And as we grow closer to him, we can begin to see the direction He wants for our lives. He is waiting.

"Then I will give them a heart to know Me, that I am the Lord; and they shall be My people, and I will be their God, for they shall return to Me with their whole heart."

Jeremiah 24:7

Reflections

1. What traditions do you cling to that interfere with your worship and prayer?

   _____

   _____

   _____

   _____

2. What / How are you hearing from God today?

   _____

   _____

   _____

   _____

3. What is your personal prayer for today?

   _____

   _____

   _____

   _____

   _____

Prayer Day 18

"having wiped out the handwriting of requirements that was against us, which was contrary to us. And He has taken it out of the way, having nailed it to the cross. Having disarmed principalities and powers, He made a public spectacle of them, triumphing over them in it. So let no one judge you in food or in drink, or regarding a festival or a new moon or sabbaths, which are a shadow of things to come, but the substance is of Christ."

Colossians 2:14-17 NKJV

Gracious Lord, forgive us when we hold fast to traditions, practices, and old laws that stifle our connection to you. Thank you for reminding us that the "requirements" were nailed to the cross with our sins and Christ arose triumphant overall. Please continue to bless us with your grace and mercy. In Jesus' name we pray and praise. *Amen.*

Reflections

1. What "requirements" in life are preventing you from truly working in your gifts of service?

   _____

   _____

   _____

   _____

2. What / How are you hearing from God today?

   _____

   _____

   _____

   _____

3. What is your personal prayer for today?

   _____

   _____

   _____

   _____

Prayer Day 19

"Then Jesus was led up by the Spirit into the wilderness to be tempted by the devil. And when He had fasted forty days and forty nights, afterward He was hungry."

Matthew 4:1-2 NKJV

***

Glorious Father, remind us that when we are at our weakest, we can be tempted. Remind us that when we are at our weakest to turn to you. Remind us to allow you to lead us in all things. Father, we are often tempted when we are overwhelmed by life and are hungry for change, rest, or comfort. Be with us. Strengthen and encourage us as we walk through our challenges. Teach us to lean on you. In Jesus' name we pray. *Amen.*

Reflections

1. Have you had some weak moments in which you have turned to earthly vices? How can you begin to change your activities?

   _____

   _____

   _____

   _____

2. What / How are you hearing from God today?

   _____

   _____

   _____

   _____

3. What is your personal prayer for today?

   _____

   _____

   _____

   _____

   _____

Prayer Day 20

"The sun had risen upon the earth when Lot entered Zoar. Then the LORD rained brimstone and fire on Sodom and Gomorrah, from the LORD out of the heavens. So He overthrew those cities, all the plain, all the inhabitants of the cities, and what grew on the ground. But his wife looked back behind him, and she became a pillar of salt."

Genesis 19:23-26 NKJV

My Lord, Our God, we see the strength and completeness of your power. Help us, Lord, as we begin again. Guide our path back to you. Forgive us for looking back, for always turning back towards those situations, people, relationships, and _____ that you have already delivered us from. Father, help our unbelief. In Jesus' name we pray. ***Amen.***

__Hmmm...__As we are ending our fasting or prayer journey, it is our prayer that God has shown us some things that we have prayed for and some things that He needed us to see.

Now as the old things – strongholds, bad habits, _____ - are destroyed (or being destroyed) we can begin anew on God's path for our lives. No turning back.

"Brethren, I do not count myself to have apprehended; but one thing I do, forgetting those things which are behind and reaching forward to those things which are ahead, I press toward the goal for the prize of the upward call of God in Christ Jesus."

Philippians 3:13-14 NKJV

Reflections

1. As you are ending this prayer journey, what are you separating yourself from and how are you ensuring your success?

    _____

    _____

    _____

    _____

2. What / How are you hearing from God today?

    _____

    _____

    _____

    _____

3. What is your personal prayer for today?

    _____

    _____

    _____

    _____

    _____

Prayer Day 21

"Now when Daniel knew that the writing was signed, he went home. And in his upper room, with his windows open toward Jerusalem, he knelt down on his knees three times that day, and prayed and gave thanks before his God, as was his custom since early days. Then these men assembled and found Daniel praying and making supplication before his God. And they went before the king, and spoke concerning the king's decree: "Have you not signed a decree that every man who petitions any god or man within thirty days, except you, O king, shall be cast into the den of lions?" The king answered and said, "The thing is true, according to the law of the Medes and Persians, which does not alter."

Daniel 6:10-12 NKJV

Heavenly Father, thank you for all things. Father, we pray for strength. We ask for strength to continue to do what is right - to continue to serve you in difficult times. Father, remind us that you are always with us. Remind us that there will be people or circumstances that challenge our faith and our convictions. Father, we trust in you to grant us courage to be steadfast and not belligerent; courage to be patient and not impulsive; courage to be faithful and not anxious; and courage to know that whatever the outcome you are ever present. In Jesus' name we pray and await your whispers of courage and love. ***Amen.***

"Fear not, for I am with you; Be not dismayed, for I am your God. I will strengthen you, Yes, I will help you, I will uphold you with My righteous right hand."

Isaiah 41:10 NKJV

Reflections

1. As you end this prayer journey? What are you thankful for?

   _____

   _____

   _____

   _____

2. What / How are you hearing from God today?

   _____

   _____

   _____

   _____

3. What is your personal prayer for today?

   _____

   _____

   _____

   _____

   _____

Prayer Day 22 – Post Fast

"The Lord has appeared of old to me, saying: "Yes, I have loved you with an everlasting love; Therefore with lovingkindness I have drawn you."

Jeremiah 31:3 NKJV

Heavenly Father, thank you for all things - for your everlasting love and grace. Thank you for walking with us and talking with us during these 21 (or ____) days. Thank you for direction and confirmation. Help us, Lord, to remember the words you have whispered to us, the plans you have laid before us, and the_____ you have given us. Thank you, Lord, for these gifts of revelation and education. In Jesus' name we pray, praise, and we are listening. ***Amen and Amen.***

Reflections

1. What did God reveal to you and how are you going to move forward from this point?

_____

_____

_____

_____

2. What / How are you hearing from God today?

_____

_____

_____

_____

3. What is your personal prayer for today?

_____

_____

_____

_____

Epilogue

Whether you have completed a January 21-day fast, a 21-day fast in any month, or a fast of any number of days, it is my prayer that these prayers helped you focus your thoughts and energies to hear and commit to the whispers of the *Father*, the *Son*, and yes, the *Holy Spirit*.

Your fast may have included the elimination of food, drink, and/or activities. The most important thing is that you have filled that time or energy with prayer and/or focus on the next steps God has for your life.

And as this fast concludes, I pray that you have learned something about yourself, your fortitude, and your self-forgiveness. We are all purposed by God, and we can only pursue that purpose when we hear from Him.

Amen.

Reflections

_____

_____

_____

_____

_____

_____

_____

_____

_____

_____

_____

_____

_____

_____

_____

_____

_____

_____

_____

_____

3 Prayers for the Road

My Lord, Our God, be with us. Help us to realize our vices when life aggravates us. Help us to realize that food, spending, and _____ will not heal us and they are temporary fixes. You are the permanent Balm in Gilead to heal the aggravation, the agitations, the sins, and all that ails us. Father, we lay our troubles at your feet and lay our hearts in your arms. In Jesus' name we pray and breathe. ***Amen.***

My God, Our Father, continue we pray to speak to us. Continue to whisper words of encouragement to our hearts and our souls. Lead us, Lord, to give your grace forward by giving to others. We need you and we need each other to survive. In Jesus' name we pray. ***Amen***.

Thank you, Lord, for your grace and your love. Thank you for reminding us to wait on you. Sometimes things do not begin or end like we think they should. But you are faithful, and your timing is everything. Remind us, Lord, to be faithful because as you promised, you will deliver. In Jesus' name we pray. *Amen.*

What Is Your Prayer?

_____

_____

_____

_____

_____

_____

_____

And in Closing...

"Stand fast therefore in the liberty by which Christ has made us free, and do not be entangled again with a yoke of bondage."

Galatians 5:1 NKJV

Heavenly Father, thank you for all things. Thank you, Lord, for every reminder that we are free in Christ. Remind us, Lord, that life will be full of opportunities that test our resolve, which challenge our patience, and erode our trust. Thank you for reminding us that we do not have to become entangled in the bondage of despair, hopelessness, hurt feelings, feelings of betrayal, or misunderstandings. Father, you are Our Source, always. As we stand fast, in faith, and in the liberty that is your Love, we ask that you heal our hearts, bind our wounds, grant us patience, clear our minds and hearts, then lead us to our next place in life and in You. In Jesus' name we pray, release, and celebrate the next steps to come. ***Amen and thank God.***

What Is Your Prayer?

_____

_____

_____

_____

_____

_____

_____

Reflections

_____

_____

_____

_____

_____

_____

_____

_____

_____

_____

_____

_____

_____

_____

_____

_____

_____

Reflections

_____

_____

_____

_____

_____

_____

_____

_____

_____

_____

_____

_____

_____

_____

_____

_____

_____

Reflections

_____

_____

_____

_____

_____

_____

_____

_____

_____

_____

_____

_____

_____

_____

_____

_____

Scripture Index

Old Testament

New Testament

Author's Works

Why Should I Be Bound? Musings on a Journey with God (2018)

Why Should I Be Bound? Musings on a Journey with God (2018) – Large Print Edition

UnSpoken Words – A Poetry Collection (2020)

Pray, Praise and Be Encouraged - A 21-day devotional (2020)

Prayers for a Friend (2021)

Why Should I Be Bound? A Prayer Journal (2022)

To purchase visit:

www.vernetcnettles.com

www.amazon.com

About the Author

Vernet Clemons Nettles, EdD is a parent, educator, speaker and writing coach. Throughout the years, she has served in various capacities of church service. Professionally, Dr. Nettles works in the Montgomery (AL) Public School System.

Dr. Nettles is a layman who enjoys seeking Christ, researching the Word of God, and relishing in the aha moments of God's promises. Always believing in the magnificence of living a Christian life, her love of Christ is firmly rooted in the journey that ebbs and flows, and even has some cloudy days and more brilliant sunlit glorious days of God's mercy.

Let's stay connected:
    www.vernetcnettles.com
    www.vcndailypray.com

www.ingramcontent.com/pod-product-compliance
Lightning Source LLC
Chambersburg PA
CBHW051700090426
42736CB00013B/2460